" *I was considering submitting my application to run for Director of Rotary International, I needed to gather as much information as I could on a variety of Rotary subjects. In the nominating interview I suspected that a question concerning membership would be asked.*"

" *After researching several different resources, it just happened that Dr. Bill Wittich sent me a preliminary copy of this Book, 'Celebrate Differences'. I was astounded that here, in this one document, was everything I thought I needed to know about membership. Dr. Wittich cited wonderful examples. He did not dictate to the reader what should be done but rather presented membership situations that made you think about how these situations might apply to my club.*"

"*After you read this book, I am sure your thoughts will be similar to mine - everything I need to know about membership is right before my eyes!*"

Steve Snyder
Far West PETS
Instruction Chair

"*Anatomy of a Rotarian -- what makes them work and not work. This is a definitive, if not weighty tome on attracting and keeping members, especially younger ones.*"

Bill Short
DGN
District 5180

"Celebrate Differences is captivating! Awesome reality of how to address the challenges of today's culture. Thanks for sharing and putting into words, what many of us have been thinking and experiencing."

John T. Capps III
Rotary GSE Team Leader, India

"The title says it all- we need to celebrate the differences and not be afraid to recognize how generational issues drive each group and simply work our recruitment and retention with the knowledge base you offer. Club culture will likely suggest refinement in both areas and that may well hold the future of clubs and our Rotary movement."

Jerry L. Hall
Vice President (2006-2007)
Director (2005-2077)
Rotary International

*This book is dedicated to all the World-Class Rotarians
I've met in my life who continue to inspire me*

Helaine & Bruce

Yours in Rotary

Bill Witt

Editor – Andrea Pitcock

ISBN # 978-0615546735

Knowledge Transfer Publishing
8650 Heritage Hill Drive
Elk Grove, CA 95624
916-601-2485
billwittich@comcast.net

First Edition

About the Author

Dr. Bill Wittich is a speaker, consultant, and author in the field of leadership, motivation, and nonprofit management.

For the past twelve years, Bill and his wife Ann, have traveled an average of 200 days a year. Their speaking schedule has taken them to all corners of the United States and through much of Europe.

His doctorate is from the University of Southern California where he continues to serve as a mentor to graduate students in the School of Policy, Planning, and Development.

Dr. Wittich has authored seven books in the association and non-profit field.

He is Past President of the Rotary Club of Laguna Sunrise in Elk Grove, California and he serves as an Assistant Governor for District 5180. He is an instructor for membership at the Far West President-Elect Training Seminars (PETS).

They enjoy living in Elk Grove, where they enjoy cooking, collecting antiques, and learning about red wine.

CONTENTS

Introduction

All Service clubs need to state in their guiding principles that it recognizes the value of diversity.

Most service clubs have not been effective in recruiting younger members into its fold. You visit the typical club and you see the typical mix of older members, even if they have added a mix of women and ethnic diversity to its fold. This book will explore how clubs can be successful in beginning to grow its membership diversity with younger men and women.

This book will explore the issues involved in bringing diversity into your service club. This book will give you the tools to successfully recruit new members of all diversity, ethnicity, gender and age. It will encourages clubs to assess those in their communities who are eligible for membership and to endeavor to include them in their clubs. In order words, all clubs should mirror their communities in regard to diversity.

For years, in North America, clubs have strived to include a strong mix of business classifications in their mix. But until only recently have clubs worked to include gender diversity in its mix. Women are now showing up in the membership counts as clubs are realizing what the corporate world has realized. Women represent a strong leadership component in every aspect of corporate and association membership.

Many clubs are also finding that ethnic diversity brings a strong unifying component to its operation as well. Some clubs are working hard to gain a wide variety of ethnic diversity into its membership while other clubs are forming ethnic clubs. An ethnic club allows groups of ethnic diversity to feel comfortable with their culture and language in a Rotary setting.

Bringing in a younger member will require clubs to face a variety of changes in their operations.

Change is difficult for everyone and particularly difficult for Rotary clubs. Generational diversity is a unique feature of club membership and for some reason, more difficult than facing either gender or ethnic diversity. Increasing the number of younger people in a Rotary club will require a new form of recruiting.

Why are we concerned about Membership?

For one reason membership in service organizations in the United States is falling. Rotary membership in the United States dropped from its peak of 445,434 in 1996 to 375,914 in 2007, according to club officials cited in the Chicago Tribune. Membership in Rotary clubs has dropped nearly 42,000 since 1995 in the USA to 360,790 last year, says Rotary spokeswoman Elizabeth Minelli.

While all century-old service clubs are losing members for a number of reasons, the nation's three largest, Rotary, Lions', and Kiwanis are losing the most members. Lions' International membership dropped from 1.45 million in 1995 to 1.3 million this year. Kiwanis membership has dropped by 20,000 since the early 1990s. Optimists International had about 94,000 members, down from 99,000 last year.

Amos McCallum, a chairman of the past national presidents of the Benevolent & Protective Order of Elks, says his group has 900,000 members, down from 1.6 million in 1980. There are even fewer Masons today — by nearly a million — than there were in 1941 as the country came out of the Great Depression, says Richard Fletcher, executive secretary of the Masonic Service Association of North America. There are an estimated 3 million members worldwide and 1.5 million in the USA, he says, compared with more than 4 million members in the USA in 1959. The Masonic Service Association (MSA) has tracked membership figures for Masons in the United States since 1925. The numbers tell a very sad tale of the decline of one of the world's most important fraternal organizations, slowly fading away, as T.S. Elliot says, "not with a bang, but a whimper."

Over half of the associations in the United States have experienced a decline in membership in 2010

This is according to the 2010 Member Marketing Benchmark Report. It appears that the tough economy, too many competing service clubs, and all those free internet resources are making it harder to attract members.

Declining Membership

Just about 10 years ago, Tom Walker had to perform a distasteful task. He stood up at a meeting of the Auburn, IL Rotary and made a motion to disband the club. The motion passed. After 63 years, the Auburn Rotary Club was no more.

At 63 years old himself, Walker was one of the youngest members at that meeting. That was one problem. The other was that only 10 people ever came to meetings. They had tried to boost membership, including putting an ad in the local newspaper soliciting new members. Nothing worked.

Larry Thompson is Past District Governor of Rotary District 6460. It's a large district that includes much of central, western and southern Illinois. Thompson says the district's membership is stable but not where he would like it to be. "It's a struggle this year with the economy," he says.

"Memberships sometimes get paid by the businesses of the members. With the economy the way it is, some of those businesses have stopped paying their employees' dues and, consequently, the employees opt not to be members."

When Vince Long joined the Lincoln Veterans of Foreign Wars post in the late 1960s, the group held meetings twice a month, had fish fries every Friday and bingo every Monday. Four decades later, the fish fries and bingo are a thing of the past, and the group meets only once a month. A couple of months ago, it even looked like Cronin Brothers VFW Post 1756 wouldn't be able to meet its mortgage and would have to close. A fundraiser saved the post in the short term, but its long-term future remains a challenge. "We use to have something going on every Friday and Saturday night," Long said. "Then, it got to where people started passing away. Things slowly went downhill." Last year, Post 1756 had about 215 dues-paying members. This year, the number is down to 188. Some of the former members quit paying dues, others moved away, and some died.

According to Kiwanis One, The Kiwanis National Newsletter, Lions and Kiwanis clubs, Shriners and other service organizations are pondering their futures as membership dwindles and average ages grow older.

Younger people are not replacing longtime members, who are finding it more difficult to summon the strength to continue with their many fundraisers

Pike Township Lions Club President David Straughn estimated that membership is down by more than half from the club's 1960s glory days, with members averaging age 70. Many once-popular club events, such as the Country Fair in Pike, are gone because of a lack of volunteers and the lessened ability of members to endure the physical labor required.

Joedy Isert, spokesman for Northwestside-based Kiwanis International, said that while there has been a slight uptick in membership in the past couple of years, overall totals have been dropping steadily for several years. The Masonic Service Association tells us in their Freemason publication that it is at its lowest membership level in at least 80 years. Even at their membership's lowest point in 1941, which included the Depression years, Freemasonry still had 800,000 more members than they do today.

When Bob Stancomb of the Galesburg Moose Lodge, says there is a huge problem with getting young people to join, he is not exaggerating. *"Let me put it to you this way,"* said Stancomb. *"I am 68 and I am one of the youngest members."* The Moose Lodge in Galesburg is not alone in facing a membership crisis. Membership at the Moose Lodge in Galesburg is down about 30 percent this year from last year. He said the club currently has about 200 members. *"Many of us are just too old,"* lamented Stancomb, Moose Lodge administrator. Declining membership could force the Moose Club to eventually relinquish its charter, a harsh reality for many long time lodge member.

"The way this is going, the club is going to just die out as people keep dying and no new people join."

Who is to Blame for this Declining Membership?

While you can blame the current economy for this declining membership, there appears to be many reasons for this loss. Let's discuss why this is happening, and what can be done to stop it. The Economy is certainly an issue for many current and potential members. But there are other concerns that we need to address for this loss of membership growth.

In *Bowling Alone*, Robert Putnam makes a powerful argument that in the last several decades of the twentieth century, all sorts of community groups and in particular, service clubs have begun to fade. Putnam states that ...

" It wasn't so much that old members dropped out, at least not anymore rapidly than age and the accidents of life had always meant. But community organizations were no longer continuously revitalized, as they had been in the past, by freshets of new members."
Robert Putnam

So why are you not recruiting a freshet of new members? Is it because you are not asking anyone to join our service club? Are you being lazy about finding prospects? Do you just fail to focus on membership? Or, is it because you are just too busy with our professional lives to remember about our membership needs. Is it really someone else's job to bring in those new members? Many members may feel that they don't recruit because they are not on the membership committee.

When you discuss the loss of service club members, particularly among younger members, it is simply a lack of knowledge that the clubs even exist. The younger prospects parents joined because it was expected by their employers, most of which paid for the membership. Today's younger prospects do not even know what a service club does. This may be partly because you fail to market your club to these younger prospects. You do not talk about your club at college business classes or at chambers of commerce.

Your reaction to a declining membership might be that you will send out an e-mail blast and expect new members to flock in the door. Or you take the issue to the board and expect the membership committee to get busy and round up those new members. To tell you the truth, while both of those solutions might help, neither will solve the overall problem. It is time for the organization to take a look at the overall issue. It is not a matter of pushing harder or getting members to accept responsibility for recruiting. It will require change in the structure of the club and believe me, that is not easy. Not only is the loss of members an issue but if you lose enough members you have the serious risk of losing the club itself.

Not only is membership dropping in all service clubs in the United States, the number of service clubs are also dropping. The Wisconsin Jaycees at the end of 2008 dissolved the Janesville Jaycees charter, which dated to the 1930s, because the club didn't have enough members.

Back in 1994 there were 8700 Rotary clubs in the United States, but now, there are less than 7700 clubs. Even as we charter new service clubs, we are facing a serious loss of clubs across the United States. Rotary requires that a club have a minimum of twenty-five members to charter. But many clubs drop down to a much smaller number of members than that before the district considers pulling their charter.

One major concern is just how small you allow a club to reach and how this small size might effect the recruiting of new members.

There appears to be a "magic" number of members for a club to function well. We simply do not know this "magic" number. It appears to differ club by club. What we do know is that service clubs take on community service projects and that requires a significant number of members. A loss of members might mean taking on less service projects or at least slowing down the rate of service. Since one of the main reasons members join a service club is to perform community service, less service projects might lead to retention problems.

Many of the issues involved in recruiting new members into service clubs are unique when bringing younger members into the club. Younger people are not replacing the older club members as they retire or pass away. It might be that the younger people in the community are already volunteering with their church and children's youth activities. It will help if we take the time right now to explore the different generations and look at what each generation requires from a service club.

Generations

As you visit service clubs it becomes apparent that the club members are aging and while that by itself is not a main issue, since all of us are aging. The real issue is that we are not been recruiting younger members into their ranks.

The same issues with generational diversity that has been creating issues in corporate America has finally shown its head in our service clubs

Corporate America finds that dealing with age diversity means understanding and relating effectively with people who are different than you. For the first time, the workplace, just like the service clubs, have four distinct generations working side by side. These four generations differ on a number of major issues including how they approach work, work/life balance, loyalty, and authority. It is time to begin to explore exactly what these differences mean and how we can begin to bridge these generations for the service clubs.

Understanding Rotary Generations

Only a few years ago, service club members were men in their professional prime, usually over 50 years of age. Most of the younger professionals would consider service club membership at a later point in their careers. Now we are attempting to grow membership from all generations. It is important to understand the differences between generations and how it impacts the recruiting of new members. Today, most service clubs are focusing considerable attention on generational differences. It appears that these differences will have important implications for the core structure of service clubs. Kiwanis took a hard look around and saw times, needs, and people changing, and decided to change with them according to Joedy Isert Northwestside-based Kiwanis International spokesman.

Jamie Notter, in his blog on association membership, *Get Me Jamie Notter*, tells us that,

> *"Different generations may reach different conclusions about what it means to be a volunteer or what value can be derived from being a part of the association at all."*

The following quote came from *The Association Renewal Blog*, which tells us they offer a random, yet compelling thoughts on next generation leadership in the association community. *"I suspect that many people under the age of 35 (and certainly under the age of 30) view associations as organizations better suited to meeting the needs of their parents' or grandparents' generations than their own. Among many people, young and old alike, associations enjoy a reputation for being rigid, highly centralized bureaucracies with a deeper commitment to defending the past and preserving the status quo than to creating the future."*

It is change that is creating most of the stress in service clubs as the traditions are being challenged and many of the good old ways of doing things are threatened. In the February 2004 issue of The Rotarian, Rester Samse, a member of RI's Membership Development and Retention Committee said...

" It helps us really, truly be a part of the family of Rotary by acknowledging that when so many different people come together, so many things happen."

It appears that Samse feels that each generation brings something unique to the table. Sam Greene in the same

Rotarian article says that *"when we put older members with the younger members, they really feed off each other."*

The blog *America's Best Business Practices* gives us an important statement about generational diversity when they said, *"It is often difficult for people of different ages to understand each other.*

A member of the Rotary Club of Vancouver Chinatown, BC, Canada gives us an interesting view about younger members...

"If a club wakes up one morning and discovers they're old, it can almost be too late."

Let's take a quick look at the four generations in the average service club and I think you will begin to understand the changes beginning to show up in your service club audiences.

The Mature Generation...The Standard Bearer

Many members are in the Mature generation, somewhat older that 65 years old. This generation might be called the traditional generation, the silent generation, or as Tom Brokaw called them, "the Greatest Generation." This is a term originally coined by Walker Smith and Ann Clurman for their 1997 book,

Rocking the Ages. This generation, born prior to 1946, currently comprises some 63 million people within the U.S. population. This generation is decreasing in the workplace due to retirement, but they are continuing to show up for their service club meetings. This is the group that has given your club its brand and a solid place in the volunteer world.

Rotary International started over 100 years ago when Paul Harris formed the first club in Chicago. Even though Paul, and his four friends that formed Rotary were in their early forties, the majority of Rotarians today are in the mature generation.

Most of them joined when they were in middle age and they are now in their sixties or older. This graying of your members has given the clubs an older appearance that the younger audience notices. These matures, in many cases are the past district governors and certainly the past presidents of most clubs. This status gives these seniors a large amount of influence both at the club level and higher up in the district levels.

Let's start by exploring just what are the characteristics of this mature generation of members. These matures grew up during World War II and most of them served in the armed forces and saw overseas duty during their military careers. If they did not personally experience the Great Depression, certainly they heard about it every time they asked their parents to purchase something for them.

They experienced this financial insecurity, either through their parent's eyes, or when they stayed too long on the telephone. The economy was booming following the war as the men were returning from their service commitment, and using the GI bill to get back to school and work.

By this point service clubs like Rotary, Kiwanis and Lions were well established and becoming very important to those up and coming white-collar executives. It was the perfect way to meet other businessmen and it lead to strong fellowship and many business opportunities. All of these service clubs were generally held over lunch where business men, all in suits and ties, would meet over a plate of chicken, sing songs, and a listen to a weekly business speaker.

These men were full of promise and optimism, for them the world was heading in the right direction. Their service club was their place of respect and they shared their stories, both war and business, during this meeting. It was only men that were allowed to join most clubs and these men enjoyed that opportunity to gather without any women present.

These mature members represented most of the successful corporations, many of which were modeled after military models. These men tended to be respectful of authority and comfortable in hierarchy and they saw value in stability. They believed, and still do, that money was an important motivator. Their club was a statement to them of their achievement and was an affirmation to themselves of their success.

Many service club matures are still employed or have, in some cases, even returned to the labor force. They may have gone back due to the current difficult economy, or simply out of boredom with that rich promise of retirement. Many tried retirement and took the cruise or purchased that RV and found it lacking in satisfaction.

For many members, community service is an opportunity to take the bull by the horns and work in their communities. They wait for that weekly meeting and are proud to let others know that they have maintained their "perfect attendance." If they must miss a meeting, they will be sure to "make-up" by attending another club meeting. Even when they travel out of town, they will make up to retain that important "perfect attendance" record and receive club recognition for it.

Their weekly meeting might begin with a song that reflects

their early days and might end by being fined for not wearing their club pin. To an older members, preserving the status of perfect attendance is a true mark of honor. To the mature member, the meeting is an every week activity and they mark their calendars to insure that they do not miss a meeting. These members are a part of the Greater Generation. They are still optimistic, affluent, and idealistic. The one thing that is clear about this generation of members is that they are loyal. They are loyal to their club and are strong believers in the club message, and they are very slow to change.

Clubs will need to continue to recruit and work even harder to retain this generation. Even as clubs talk about bringing in younger members, everyone is aware that this mature generation represents the history and finance of the traditional club.

These older members might be slightly less able to work on community projects, but they are still able to support them financially. Younger members might have careers, families and responsibilities that create stumbling blocks for their club careers. But these mature members have lived through all those empty nesting years and are still strongly connected to their club.

One of the many strengths of the mature member, is their solid connection to the club.

These mature members are very productive as volunteers, and even more so, are able to support their club with dollars. They strongly value their fellowship and have a strong desire to work on community activities. When you consider how to recruit matures, it is generally one mature recruiting another mature.

Once the new member gets into the club and sees the strong fellowship, it becomes a quick decision to stay. The best technique for recruiting matures is face to face. They enjoy a personal relationship with fellow matures. This generation has time available to devote to community activities. They will generally tell you that being retired gives them the time to become a club leader. They say that prior to retirement they did not have freedom to carry on the duties related to governance. Because of both this extra time and many times extra dollars, we need to search for retired prospects for club membership.

Where Do You Find These Matures?

Matures are found in multiple locations around town. Good recruiting locations are the community senior center and their place of faith. It is a spot where one member would have an opportunity to meet and greet other matures and tell the club story. The value of both locations is that these people already have the spirit of community connection and giving back. But it will take a person of about the same age to be able to sit down with that mature, and sharing a cup of coffee, talk about what Rotary means to them.

It is really more sharing your love for Rotary, than attempting to sell Rotary.

People catch your enthusiasm, and they like that fire inside you, and how it shows your passion about Rotary. We know the increased life expectancy today is due to the improvements in health care, and matures have many more years that they can use in community service. This generation grew up with a strong belief in service. It started with the war environment and continued throughout their lives.

Ken Dychtwald, author of Age Wave, informs us that matures are *"more comfortable with the hierarchies prevalent early in their careers, and some may struggle to adjust to today's more fluid, flattened and networked enterprises."*

Matures enjoy that face-to-face meeting when you sit down with them to explain the opportunity to join your service club. It is that in-person meeting that sparks that interest in finding out about your club. The mature is moving slowly into the connected environment of the internet, but be slow in offering it to them as a recruiting tool.

Many younger people feel that matures lack interest in the newer social media technologies. The truth is that matures are the fastest growing audience for Facebook. As stated in *Inside Facebook*, a web site devoted to tracking Facebook users,

"Facebook has been growing rapidly amongst people over 55 in the US"

Facebook itself will tell you that the 55 years and over is the fastest growing internet demographic group. The important thing to understand about matures is that they are very willing to continue to improve their skills and are willing to stretch their talents.

Social networking is on the rise with this generation and they are definitely not technophobic. Many Rotary clubs now have

Facebook pages and even Facebook Fan pages.

In many cases, these pages are being designed by mature Rotarians. A Facebook page can create a great many opportunities for your club online. Therefore, more and more clubs are migrating to Facebook from more traditional, less manageable platforms such as static websites.

Retention is a major concern for many clubs. But it is not the mature generation that is slipping out the back door. They are the least likely to terminate their membership, with the exception of illness or death. Once they join, they stay.

One danger to watch out for in your club is over-stressing the desire to recruit younger members.

Yes, the growth of service clubs must include bringing in 30 and 40 year olds, but avoid excluding the recruitment of outstanding mature members. I think we do that without intending to upset any of our mature members, but they easily sense that we are discounting their value, as we push so hard to find those younger members.

Just this week I had one of our senior members complain that the new push for younger members is discounting the value of our senior members. They take it very personally when we talk about needing younger members. They sense that we are no longer looking for mature members, which is not at all true. Remember that it is our mature members that support their clubs through their history and perfect attendance. They are the ones who show up for every event and who take out their check books first when you ask for Foundation dollars. They are the majority of our Past District Governors and many of the Past Presidents of clubs. They may qualify for the 85 Rule, which says that you don't count them absent if their age and years in Rotary add up to at least 85. But even the 85 Rule members are the ones continuing their perfect attendance status.

Boomers

Baby Boomers, the generation of 78 million Americans born between 1946 and 1964, represent a potential boom to the Rotary world. This generation is the largest and most powerful consumer group ever. The term "baby boom" was coined by Landon Jones for his 1980 book, *Great Expectations*. This boomer generation has had a significant influence on every aspect of society due to their generation's size of 77 million.

The largest number of members in clubs today tends to be Boomers

These are our members who are over 40 and in many cases just turning 65 years old. This dynamic, historic generation is an agent of change. They may have started off the 1960's as protesters and rebels, but they have invented their own world and have refined things in the 1970's and '80s. Boomers are a very large generation and these numbers continue to impact all service clubs. They followed the mature generation and in many ways copied their values and work ethic. But they spend their incomes passionately, spending on children, grandchildren, and Rotary.

Boomers and Retirement

Boomers spent years talking about retirement, but once they got to the magic retirement age they said no. They might take that pension and then go right back into the labor market. They might start their own business, or just work part-time, but work they will not give up. They will also not get old.

According to author Gronbach in his book The Age Curve, *"the American Association for Retired People (AARP) decline in membership over the past ten years should have been a clue."*

This clue is that they are not yet ready to even consider full retirement. Nearly two out of three baby boomers admit to worrying about retirement, and most expect to continue working beyond age sixty-five. What's more, that number will continue to grow for many years to come, as the youngest Baby Boomers will not reach age 65 until 2029. There will be 10,000 boomers retiring everyday until the year 2030.

This is the generation that choose to work. Work was the most important thing in their lives.

They are a driven generation. Work was the way they gained their reputation. The question in a boomer group was always, "Glad to meet you, what do you do?" They got to travel earlier and further that any generation before them. They were better educated than their parents and were the last generation to be more successful than their parents.

Boomers as Workaholics

They bought in large numbers and spent money on pleasure items. As a large generation, they learned to compete with each other for the jobs they desired. They were the first generation to wear the term "workaholic." Ten-hour workdays and putting off their vacations, became a standard operating practice for these boomers.

Boomers lives are exciting, productive, yet hectic and overextended. They are still trying to do it all. They are juggling careers and being both parents, and grandparents. Boomers are beginning to think travel, be it taking a cruise, buying an RV, or purchasing a timeshare.

There is a lot of "me" in the boomers outlook toward life. Watching their cash flow, while watching their savings disappear from the fall of the stock market makes for a confused boomer. They want to pay down their debts, while at the same time finally slow down and enjoy their lives.

They are at a point where their children are mostly out of the house and off to college, but many fear that these children might return home after college. Many boomers are part of the "sandwich generation", paying that expensive college tuition for their children, and at the same time paying for equally expensive elder care for their parents.

Boomers as Rotarians

As Rotarians, these boomers are mostly in charge of their clubs. They out-number every other generation, and they let everyone know that. They are past presidents in most cases, and continue to serve on their board of directors. They control the club budget, and by doing that, they control where the money goes. They are attending international conventions in large numbers, and work to make it a vacation to boot. At the convention, they enjoy all those host trips and after-convention tours.

At Rotary meetings, boomers sit together and become a club-within-a-club.

Younger members may have a difficult time breaking into this fold of boomers. Boomers do not see that as an issue since they certainly have paid the dues to get their prime spot in the club. And after all, they are the past presidents and PDGs aren't they? In many cases, they have slowed down on the hands-on work, and are beginning to write checks to cover their involvement.

When you talk about membership recruiting, boomers are still active, but slow at bringing in new members. Those that they bring in are usually clones of themselves. In other words, mature men bringing in other mature men.

John Maxwell, in his classic leadership text, *The 21 Irrefutable Laws of Leadership*, calls it The Law of Magnetism. Maxwell says that good leaders are always on the lookout for good people and that each of them carries around a mental list of what kind of people they would like to have in their club.

Boomer club members are those leaders and I believe that each of them has in mind the kind of person they want in their club. Maxwell asks an interesting question about this and also has an interesting answer. He asks, *"...what will determine whether the people you want are the people you get, and whether they will have the qualities you desire?"* He says that you will be surprised by this answer. Believe it or not,

"Who you get is not determined by what you want. It's determined by who you are"

John is suggesting that you will always bring into our club people who possess the same qualities you do. That's the Law of Magnetism. Who you are, is who you attract. In other words, Leaders draw people to them who are like themselves.

That means you are recruiting people of the same age, same attitude, and same values that you possess. The Law of Magnetism is powerful. Whatever character you possess, you will likely find it in the people who follow you into the club. This is not a bad thing. Boomers are great club members. You know what a club member should look like and act like. If the people boomers bring into the club are just like them, then we end up with more outstanding club members.

But, and it seems there is always a but in everything we do. If you see value in attracting younger people to our clubs, this "law of magnetism" may be an issue. We will need to work on boomers to insure that they see the value in bringing younger members into their clubs.

Boomers Are Not Leaving

The good news about boomers is that they are not leaving their service clubs. Marc Freedman, founder of the Experience Corps, the country's largest national service program for American's over fifty-five agrees that boomers are not going to fade softly into the night. They are active, healthy and expect to live to ninety and beyond. Even those who retire will look for a second career and will do it by finding those things that they had put onto their "bucket list" the first time around.

Many will change their focus from a concern about income, to a concern about doing something meaningful. This is where the service club fills many of their meaningful spaces. Many boomers will find that their volunteering is being done through community and international service. You will find these boomers working in the local park on a club project or taking off for Mexico to build homes as part of an international project.

Boomers will stay Young

It is extremely important to boomers that they stay young. Faith Popcorn, the marketing expert for the New York Times, says that,

> *"Boomers are redefining middle age because they are really trying to stay young."*

They are walking for exercise or going to the gym to work out, all to keep their bodies in shape to exist in a healthy mode for the next thirty years. Boomers are also searching for that healthy diet and are moving toward anything that promises a long life with quality. Daniel Kadlec, a columnist for Time magazine tells us that,

"33 percent of boomers are volunteering and that is while they are still in their working years."

One of the reasons that Rotary gets so much volunteer help from boomers and mature members is that it treats them with respect. Too often, a volunteer nonprofit agency assumes that these older volunteers can only do "envelope stuffing" and other menial tasks. The volunteer gets insulted and never returns. But Rotary assumes, correctly, that the members will jump in with both feet and bring their wallets and purses along as well.

Offering these boomers an opportunity to do meaningful volunteer work, along with strong fellowship and a chance to use their skills is a key to recruiting them. Rotary stresses that the club is the cornerstone of Rotary, where the most meaningful work is carried out. It also tells us that Rotarians will get out of Rotary what they put into it. Remember that boomers grew up believing that they were going to change the world. They are the generation that did alter much of our corporate landscape.

Boomers and Technology

While they didn't invent the computer, they certainly picked up that technology and ran with it. Bill Gates from Microsoft is a boomer, as is Steve Jobs from Apple. As boomers entered the workforce in the seventies, the technological revolution was just getting underway. But it was the boomers who jumped on it and helped to create the digital revolution.

Boomers changed the world from typing to keyboarding, from sending snail mail to e-mail, from pay phone to cell phone.

But even these boomers are becoming less driven now, then they were in their thirties and forties. They are now leaders, members of the establishment, even grandparents. But they are still very much boomers. People may age and change but they still hold to their generational underpinnings.

It is important to remember that boomers are basically team players, and very service-oriented. They are always willing to go the extra mile and are very good at building and maintaining relationships. They are not comfortable with conflict and go out of their way to avoid it. If they sense that their club is in conflict, they are likely to avoid those people or even stop attending meetings. On the board they are reluctant to go against their fellow club members. So while they have strong leadership ability, they prefer to avoid arguements which they see as hurting relationships. Boomers still have a "workaholic personality", but today you will sense they are beginning to seek more work/life balance.

Even as they slow down, boomers do not want to release their status, which was conferred by their work position.

Even in Rotary, the boomer hangs on to their work position by wearing it on their badge as a "classification" symbol. Rotary tells us that "by assigning each member a classification, based on his or her business or profession, this system ensures that the club's membership reflects the business and professional composition of its community."

They further state that this classification principle "enlivens the club's social atmosphere and provides a rich resource of occupational expertise to carry out service projects and provide club leadership." It is important to realize just how important this listing of a member's classification really is. Clubs check with the new member to get it correct. It is particularly important to the boomer since "who they are or have been" is the essence of their professional being.

You will find that very few boomers wish to carry the title "retired" unless it is followed by their prior professional classification. One individual that I brought into my club recently, told me that even though he is retired, he would prefer to have "Supervisor, General Construction" on his name badge. In fact, if I had made the decision to put "retired" on his badge, he might have made a second choice about joining the club.

Who is Bringing Boomers into Rotary?

Boomers tend to be recruited into the club by fellow boomers. They feel comfortable with someone in their own generation asking them to come and sample the club experience. The best sales approach tends to focus on fellowship and service. Many boomers, particularly when they leave their careers, are without a large number of friends. They may have friends that they enjoy for dinner or travel, but these are usually not strong buddies. Both men and women as boomers are searching for fellowship. If the club that they visit is not immediately warm and inviting, they will not stay.

Women tend to be easier at developing buddies than men, but

even these buddies, are not the friends that you do community service with. It might be that their church friends will be the ones that they perform church service with, but it is generally not community service and hardly ever international service.

Women boomers will be hesitant to attend a Rotary club unless another boomer woman does the ask.

Generally it is another woman of the same generation that is most successful. Maybe it is just that we feel more comfortable with people who have more similarities than differences.

Even men will tend to attract other men with similar traits, and that is the one they ask to come to Rotary. Think for a minute about those people who you have invited to a Rotary meeting. I bet that these people have a similar attitude to you. You seldom see people with a positive attitude attracted to those with a negative attitude. You also probably asked others who were of roughly the same age. And you tend to ask people to Rotary whose values are similar to yours.

*Whatever character you possess, you will likely find in the people **you** invite to Rotary.*

Generation X Rotarians

Nearly 50 million Americans carry the tag "Gen X." Generation X, is the generation waiting for the boomers to retire, and in many cases have already become the boomer's boss. Gen Xers were born between 1965 and 1980.

Many attribute this term to a novel written by Douglas Copeland and published in 1990, which he titled Generation X. This generation numbers some 50 million according to the U.S. Bureau of the Census. They grew up in the decades following the boom in births. But many boomers worry that this younger generation, rather than gaining the experience at running that fundraising event, will want to lead it and dismiss the boomers' suggestions to learn before taking leadership roles.

According to Sarah Sladek in her book, "The New Recruit" tells us that everything about this younger generation is new and different, from their values and expectations to the way they communicate and spend their time. She suggests that,

What worked in the past for associations won't work for the younger generations.

Rotary is one those membership associations. Many associations remain almost entirely governed and supported by the mature and boomer generation, and few are developing plans and strategies to bring in new and younger generations. Many of the younger generations refer to today's membership associations as outdated and irrelevant. This might be because the groups don't provide anything meaningful or relevant to them.

David Parsons of Springfield Illinois, District Governor of District 6469, says,

"Attracting the younger generation is going to mean two things — getting longtime members to embrace new ways of doing things and refocusing the traditional approach."

"Today's up-and-coming generation," he says, "is interested in service, not just sitting at a meal and chit-chatting socially. They want to be actually doing something, getting involved." David adds, "Still, you've got to keep the meetings for your older folks. I like to go to dinner meetings, get there early, chat with people. You have to do both." These Gen Xers are somewhere between 30 and 45 years old and have seen the economy go into a recession and watched the dot-com bubble burst. There are many fewer Gen Xers than boomers due to the fact that the U.S. birth rates plummeted.

Work/Life Balance

Because of Gen Xers emphasis is on life before work, boomers tend to think of them as "slackers." Boomers were the workaholics of the workplace, and then the generation that followed them has been tagged by the term, the Slacker Generation. But you have to remember that this is the generation that watched their parents get layed off, right-sized or down-sized. They did not understand or agree with what was being done to their parents. But, it is not going to happen to them.

They decided that their life was to have less pressure and be a lot more fun. They are cynical of the corporate world, and are much more family oriented. They are family oriented, maybe because they were the first generation that grew up with divorced parents, two working parents or the experience of being latchkey kids. This has caused many Gen Xers to become more involved parents.

They are referred to as the "Family-First" Generation" by USA Today.

You will see this at Rotary meetings as they bring their children to meetings. It's not because they cannot afford a sitter. It is because they want to share their children with fellow Rotarians. Men are as likely to be in charge of the households as the boomer wives were. It is a role reversal, which is enjoyed by Gen Xers. They feel that both family members should have the opportunity to raise the children and earn a living.

When you work to recruit younger members into Rotary, it is critical that the club focus on a wide variety of family activities. These are the members that are still raising their families and are very focused on family life.

Where the boomers, at that same family life stage would ask their parents to baby sit so they could go to a Rotary event, Gen Xers will bring the kids along. It is important to stress to prospective new members the ability of the club to involve family in its activities. But do not promise something that the club is unwilling to do.

Diversity is a Key to Generation X

Race, gender and sexual orientation turned from rigid identity categories to flexible markers where people crossed lines in new ways. Generation X was the first generation to become "color blind." Their friends are from any race and ethnic background. They do not view color or race as an issue. They are concerned by their parent's inability to eliminate prejudice in their conversation. They expect to see all Rotary clubs contain people of color and women in numbers that mirror the community. They also expect Rotary to be open to sexual orientation as well. That may be what lead the Rotary 2010 Council On Legislation to adopt Enactment 10-40 which states that, *"No club, regardless of the date of its admission to membership in RI, may by provisions in its constitution or otherwise, limit admission in the club on the basis of gender, race, creed, national origin or sexual orientation."*

Generation X is the fixer generation

A desire of the Gen X generation is to fix the problems they see in the world. They have been very involved in high school and college service learning programs. Many have traveled overseas on church missions or other nonprofit overseas programs.

> *Their desire for improving the world certainly makes this generation a natural connection with Rotary.*

What Rotary offers with its Polio-Plus program and dozens of other world-wide humanitarian ventures including clean water, food and health service programs puts it right on the Generation X plate.

Why is Generation X So Difficult to Recruit?

If everything we are saying about those 30-45 year old Gen Xers indicates that they are a perfect connection to Rotary, then why are they so hard to recruit? Remember that I said that this generation is skeptical and they do not trust everything the prior generations says. Put yourself in their shoes and go visit the average Rotary club. What do you see when you walk in the door? A group of older men are sitting around the table. And these men are singing some song from the 40's or earlier. They all sit together, and do not invite you to join their table? There are only a hand-full of women present and almost no one of color. Maybe there was one person under the age of 40. You are not really surprised since all your friends told you that is what you would find. They said it was their Dad's club, if not grandpa's club.

You are not surprised, since you did what comes natural to your generation, and you checked out their website. The first club you thought you might visit, did not even have a website. The one that did have a website was way out of date. You checked for the club Facebook page, but could not find one.

Younger members will join Rotary if they see the value and are provided with a sense of belonging, given adequate opportunities to contribute, and if their participation is valued.

This is asking a lot of Rotary clubs. It is asking you to consider making some changes, and change is hard. You have a fun place where you go each week to be with your friends. Friends, who by the way, are very similar to you. You brought all these people into Rotary and they are fine Rotarians. Why then should we consider changing? Many service clubs are suffering from a lack of interest from people in joining their clubs.

If Rotary is going to appeal to the younger generation, they must be able to think of themselves in a different way, which in many cases means a complete repositioning of the organization's marketing efforts.

It is interesting that most Rotary clubs are finding to easier it bring ethnic diversity into the club than age diversity. The focus group of the Membership Development Division of Rotary found that *"It might be easier to bring in ethnic diversity depending on how great the gap has become between the club's average age and the younger professionals."*

They also stated that a younger professional can be intimidated or turned-off by the formality and ritual associated with many Rotary clubs. The truth, as stated by many of the younger members, is that they are looking for a more comfortable and relaxed environment where they can have fun and still get things done. It seems to be the ritual that they object to, and they want short meetings that get more to the point and as they say, "accomplish something." They are busy between work and home responsibilities, and they don't want to attend meetings unless the club has a meaningful program.

Money, Money, Money and Gen X

Many younger professionals say Rotary is simply too expensive. They mean the dues, the cost of meals, travel, meetings, service projects and fundraising. But, it might be that the meals are the most expensive portion of expense that the young member faces.

How does a club help the young member to handle those costs associated with Rotary?

Some older members will simply say Rotary has always been a rich man's club. I know they are teasing, but there may be a little truth in the fact that people did not join Rotary until they were in their place in life where they could afford it. *"If you're fifty years old and vice president of a company, you can join a chamber of commerce. If you're twenty or thirty years old, you're not likely to join the chamber or attend $200 dinners to be social or a $25 breakfast. It's not something our age group is going to do,"* stated F. Anne Harrel, founder of the Boston Young

Professionals Association.

A few districts have suggested that clubs consider lowering the total cost of membership. They remind their clubs that some younger members are having trouble meeting the financial obligations of club membership. To combat this problem, some clubs have lowered their fees or have a meal only once or twice a month instead of every week. They also recommend that clubs consider waiving certain fees or expenses for the first year or two. Younger members who aren't yet fully invested in Rotary may be more apprehensive about committing to all of the financial obligations of club membership.

Once they become involved in your club and dedicated to Rotary's mission, they may be more willing and able to pay the full amount. Many clubs will panic at the thought of lowering dues and fees because it can have a negative budget implication. But these clubs need to be willing to take a budget loss on the dues to engage and grow a young professional with the club.

It might be that a long-term benefit outweights the short-term risk.

Millennials

The youngest of the four generations in Rotary are the Millennials, young professionals between 18 and 30. This Millennial Generation was born between 1981 and 1999. This term was originally coined by William Strauss and Neil Howe, who have written extensively on the impact of generational differences.

Millennials are 81 million strong in size and were raised by "helicopter parents," who doted on them, giving them an ample supply of attention and validation. This new group is leaving college and joining the workforce in growing numbers. Sometimes referred to as "Generation Y", or the "Net Generation," this group prefers to be called the "Millennial Generation." It is as group as large as the boomers, in fact, they make up nearly a third of the U.S. population. This is the largest generation of young people since the 1960s.

They grew up during the "digital age" and even though we think of them as technologically literate, the truth is they are technologically dependent. They cannot imagine living without their cell phones, computers, computer games, and GPS. Even though they use all of this technology, many of them do not really understand how it works.

According to *Time Magazine* (March 2010),

Over 83% of Millennials sleep with their cell phones, often checking them two or three times a night for any new text messages.

They get upset with their friends when they text them at 3 a.m. and don't receive a text message right back. This generation is connected to their parents and friends 24/7, and consult their parents before making any decision. These decisions include college, employment, living arrangements, and maybe even whether they should join Rotary. They look at websites before applying for college, employment and again, before joining Rotary. They will likely shop for a Rotary club before joining, and will make their decision based on what they see on their smart phone screen

Millennials are Volunteers

They are already engaged in their communities, in a way their parents never were. They are volunteering, raising money, and working to fight poverty, pollution, disease, and the big issues confronting the world today. Volunteering, on the part of young people, has hit an all-time high. The Higher Education Research Institute reported that some 83 percent of incoming college freshman have volunteered and over 70 percent did it on a weekly basis. The same survey found that two-thirds of college freshmen think it is very important to help other people; and about the same percentage say it is very likely they would do community service in college.

Morley Winograd in his book, *Millennial Makeover*, stated that *"... in many respects they are more like the GI Generation grandparents and great-grandparents than they are like their own parents."* Both the Mature and the Millennial generations are also large in comparison with the generations that immediately preceded their own.

The Connected Generation

Globalization and technology have been shaping change since the dawn of time. But now Millennials connect with their farthest-flung neighbors in real time, regardless of geography, through online communities of interest. Their friends are all over the world via Facebook, MySpace, Twitter, and Skype.

Millennials grew up in a "sound bite" era. Twitter, according to Wikipedia, is a social networking and microblogging service that enables its users to send and read other user messages called tweets. Tweets are text-based posts of up to 140 characters. This sound bite has become a distinguishing characteristic of the way young people communicate.

Millennials are using their social networking sites to further their volunteer efforts. Ron Alsop in his book *The Trophy Kids Grow Up*, tells us about a start-up called Project Agage, using the social network site Facebook to launch the Causes program with the goal of empowering individuals.

"Facebook users are being encouraged to recruit their network of friends to support their pet cause."

Of all of the talents that Millennials bring to the workplace, being technologically savvy is their greatest skill contribution. They are constantly connected as they listen to their iPods or send text messages, all while working on a critical project. Social media is at the heart of their world. This allows them to connect with co-workers and friends around the world at great speed. The electronic capabilities of Millennials are extraordinary.

Your club website and Facebook page are the primary locations that younger people go to find out about your club. If it is out of date or appears boomer-centric, they will pass. In a Facebook page from Rotary International, which asked questions concerning how younger people might advise Rotary Clubs about attracting new people, one younger Rotarian said,

"A major mistake of clubs is not to invest any time in keeping websites up to date and interesting"

This is the first place people will go to when they are searching for a club - and if there is nothing there or it looks boring, that would be a big minus.

The Rotary Club of Milwaukee is working hard these days to stay technologically relevant 95 years after it was founded. *"The view is that service organizations are dead and membership is dying,"* says Mary McCormick, executive director of the Rotary Club of Milwaukee. *"We're constantly holding up the mirror to figure out how to continue to be relevant."*

It is important to realize that Rotary International has a presence on Facebook, Twitter and LinkedIn and sponsors discussion groups on those sites.

Millennials are Green

This generation is not turning green, they are green, very concerned about the environment, and willing to volunteer to save it. According to a survey by Cone and Amp Insights, *"nearly 80% of millennials say they prefer to work for a company that cares about making contributions to society."* If this generation turns out to the most generous generation as the literature makes it seem is possible, they will be perfect for Rotary.

> *"Their desire to do volunteer work, both in their local communities, and even to take on global challenges, makes them a dead ringer for Rotary membership."*

U.S. President Barack Obama expressed satisfaction that young people are much more aware and focused about environmental issues than his generation. This interest in the environment is a natural connection for young people and Rotary. Since 1905, Rotary members worldwide have implemented thousands of environmental projects, from digging wells and creating conservation areas to starting community recycling programs. This started to grow during the Rotary year 2008-09 with the birth of a revitalized "green movement" within Rotary. Even though millennials are known to be the most environmentally educated generation, they often do not take action on their extensive knowledge, which is a strong reason to get connected with this younger generation. Rotary might supply the vehicle for their volunteer movement.

A new Rotary club spanning the border between Minnesota and Wisconsin has put a focus on helping the environment while reaching out to younger members. The Rotary Club of Duluth Superior Eco has adopted a decidedly ecological theme in both name and service projects. Each month, the club participates in projects that focus on making a positive impact on the environment or local community. Past projects have included pulling buckthorn at a local nature center and helping a theater company organize its script library.

Amy Haney was the 2010-2011 Duluth Superior Eco Club President and she tells us *"This Club truly fits my lifestyle as I am a hands-on person who cares about our environment. Our club members have a commitment to hands on, environmentally friendly service projects*

Membership Issues

Recruiting Younger Members

The Newsletter for Rotary District 1170 said it clearly, "Historically, Rotary has always been an elitist organization to which people wanted to belong. In today's busy world that is no longer the case, and potential members in the community need to be identified and nurtured.

> *"In most cases young people will not beat a path to your door."*

Years ago, when you were in a certain business you almost had to belong to a service club to be successful, but it's not that way anymore. Business support has waned. In many companies the difficult economy is eliminating company payment of membership dues. It was standard practice to have upper management employees belong to the key service clubs in town. Past Rotary Director Ron Beaubien said Rotary and other traditional service organizations, including Jaycees, Kiwanis, and Lions, are losing members even though volunteerism is on the rise among 25- to 54-year-olds. He calls for "progressive" changes that will give Rotary a more flexible structure to attract younger people with busy lives. Beaubien said,

"Younger members will not join boring Rotary clubs that just meet and eat,"

Jim Henry, membership coordinator from Rotary Zone 34 said *"Unless I mistake its seriousness, the membership decline in North American Rotary clubs needs, no, demands bold persistent experimentation in order to reverse course. To pursue new and retain existing members by doing the same thing over and over again expecting different results is lunacy. Common sense says to try different approaches. If the different approach doesn't work, admit it and try something else. But above all, try something!"*

The blog titled *Grow Your Business* written by Russell White speaks to why Rotary Clubs are losing membership. It says "Rotary groups have an attendance requirement and a rigid schedule of meetings. Whites states,

"This is what is wrong with these groups: the model no longer fits the business world"

White goes on to say, *"Today's business world is fluid, leaders are schedule challenged, and people only want to pay for exactly what they want and attend only those meetings that interest them. Remember buying an entire album or CD for the one or two songs on it you really liked? Today young people pay by the song, when they want it, 24/7. No more paying for what you don't want to hear and no more waiting on store hours to buy it. Business gatherings are now the same way."* He further states that, *"the younger generation of upcoming leaders are more expense focused, more immediate results oriented and more mobile. They do not identify as closely to their geographic location, traveling freely for business and pleasure and often working for companies hundreds of miles away."*

He states flatly that,

"If Rotary Clubs want to increase involvement and attendance of younger, more active leaders, they need to create better programs and drop membership requirements"

Rotary is almost entirely governed and supported by the Baby Boomer and mature generation and few clubs are developing plans or strategies to begin recruiting younger members. Bill Boyd, past Rotary International President said it best, *"Rotary will die if we don't bring in younger members."* Truly the clubs that fail to engage the younger generations will age noticeably and eventually become obsolete. Those clubs that are trying to attract younger members need to realize that young members have completely different values, interests, needs, and wants from the generations before them.

> *These younger generations will not respond to the recruiting efforts of the past.*

You cannot just add a Facebook page or blog and expect the new generations to come running. Many changes will be required to bring in younger members and the best approach is to have the entire organization embrace the changes.

Are these new young generations joiners?

When it comes to younger members, some Rotary clubs seem perplexed by this unique and dramatically different generation. These young people are not joining organizations in the numbers or with the same enthusiasm and commitment as prior generations. They are just very selective about how they spend their time and who they spend it with. Younger people have to feel a sense of trust and belonging before joining a service club.

Young people grew up in front of the television and their laptop computers. Baby Boomers like to socialize and network, while younger members prefer meeting in small groups and communicating with e-mail. Rotary continues to focus on the weekly meeting which provides a sense of fraternity to Boomers, but does not have the same appeal to younger members. One concern that continues to show its head is that Rotary is considered by many young people as an older persons club. That is understandable since club membership does reflect a high number of over 50 year olds. We know that 89% of all Rotarians are over the age of 40.

Boomers vs Younger People

The biggest difference between younger people and boomers is what they expect to derive from their membership. Younger workers demand more of a return on their investment and are less likely to join an organization where they pay a fee without any tangible return or real participation. It is abundantly clear that young people don't join things just to be members. "They don't discharge social capital responsibility by writing a check and being a member of something. That's characteristic of a past generation." according to Arthur Brooks, PhD, director of the Nonprofit Studies Program at the Maxwell School of Citizenship and Public Affairs at Syracuse University.

Paul Kiser in his blog on Rotary tells us that *"Rotary was truly a young professionals networking club at its inception; however, today's Rotary club is a foreign environment to most business people under 45."* He says that *"Interestingly, in discussions with Rotarians I have found we often have no clue as to how young professionals perceive Rotary, and in fact, I have found that some Rotarians have a bias against youth."* It is not a good thought and we all hope that this is not true. But Paul found that in one case a very prominent local Rotarian was advising clubs to ignore anyone under 40 as a potential member. His reasoning was that, *"They have kids and they're not in a place in their career to be a good Rotarian."* Paul said, *"that was a great attitude...for keeping Rotary an old person's organization."*

A Sense of Community

To attract younger members, Rotary will have to think about providing services and creating a sense of community. One way to accomplish this is by being a resource for members' career development, offering programs and services to help at every stage of their working life through retirement.

We need to remember that this younger generation is changing both jobs and careers on an everyday basis. Research indicates that the average young employee changes jobs every 1.3 years.

This certainly affects the membership in service clubs as these young members change jobs and locations. That is a challenge to building a sense of community as your members relocate on a continual basis.

It appears that younger members are typically less comfortable in social settings than Baby Boomers. This could be a result of the dramatic changes featured in their work lives. It is certainly more difficult to have the club be relevant to their careers and to their communities. Chuck Underwood, founder of The Generational Imperative tells us that,

"Clubs must earn younger members attendance by making the meeting relevant to their careers and their lives."

The young person spends more time volunteering for worthy causes than any generation before them. A study done in 2006 by the Cone Marketing Forum showed that *"61% of Millennials feel personally responsible for making a difference in the world."* But the key is that if Rotary does not fight for these young people, they will lose them.

The key will be how flexible we can be with the limited amount of time that this audience has to give. We also must realize that young members will only volunteer if the work is meaningful and if they can have input. You must understand that the young people will have time there for the taking, but only if you approach them in the right way. They will only share their time with organizations they figure are in synch with their values and that offer them an opportunity to create meaningful experiences.

Time, Money, and Family Concerns

Three major issues confronting younger people as they consider joining a service club is time, money and family. They feel that their time is impacted by both work needs and family responsibilities. These three issues usually come up during recruiting talks with potential members. They will ask questions relating to how much time is expected of members, how much money does Rotary expect, and how can my family be involved in Rotary activities.

Time might be impacted by the age of the potential member and their place in the work world. For example, if the Rotarian is older and already retired, then the time concerns are not as critical. But if the young member is working longer hours or even working at more than one job, it will be a major concern. If the couple has small children needing lots of care and transportation, then time again becomes a major concern. As younger women move into Rotary, childcare usually takes a major role in the time arena. If both mom and dad are working, then childcare becomes an even stronger issue. It appears that time and the apparent lack of it in today's busy world of work and pleasure is a major issue.

With the growth of single moms and single dads, childcare issues become even stronger.

Time is an issue as the club requires a weekly meeting for continuing membership in the club. There are options that clubs might consider in relationship to the time concerns. They might hold meetings less frequently than weekly or simply overlook weekly attendance requirements. Rotary has changed its meeting requirements to only 50% attendance requirements of weekly meetings. It has launched e-clubs that allow members to meet on their home or office computers, either by joining a Rotary Club that meets only through electronic media or as a way to make up when you miss your weekly Rotary meeting.

Money is another issue for many, even without considering the current economy. Rotary has always been considered a rich person's game, even if that was a false perception. But still it does require funding for both annual dues and weekly meals at the Rotary club. There is pressure in some clubs to pay fines and to contribute to the Rotary Foundation. While this is optional, it might still increase the pressure for those with limited incomes. There are options for clubs to cut the expense of meals by substituting less expensive meals or offering an option to not have a meal.

Even early morning meetings at Starbucks might be an alternative. A few clubs give up the meals all together and go to a happy-hour format where purchasing a drink is optional. It is a matter of the club trying to fit in to the members' lifestyles. Rotary District 5170 in their Membership Minute illustrated this point by suggesting two possible solutions to help younger members. They suggest that a club might consider lowering the total cost of membership in your club. They might consider waiving certain fees or expenses for the first year or two.

Family activities may require a majority of time and money for many younger members. Since the family requires so much more in the way of classes and sports activities these days, it is a trade-off for many prospective members.

Rotary clubs are beginning to see that their members want to volunteer with their families and kids.

Younger people want their children to get involved and get their hands dirty volunteering with mom and dad. But it takes the club to planning ahead and taking on service projects that allow full family involvement. Young people want to build houses and playgrounds. They love the concept of Habitat for Humanity and the Rotary House for families with children in a hospital. It may be that the concept of family clubs with both husbands and wives joining the same club along with childcare might become a viable option.

Tom Cross from the Davis Sunrise Rotary gives a few very insightful comments concerning today's Rotarian and the idea of family. *"I see Rotary & Family as just the tip of the iceberg. The family dynamic has and is changing from when Rotary started. My impression of early Rotarian's Family was made up of one single income and a spouse at home taking care of the family, cooking, and supporting the Rotarian. This allowed the Rotarian to devote 100% of the community service piece of the pie."* It appears that future Rotarians will have to balance family, income, time, and Rotary with all the requirements of double incomes and work/life balance.

Henry Bradley III, Past President of the Islandia-Central Islip Rotary Club in Suffolk County, Long Island, New York, states it clearly when he says, *"Our club always includes our local youths and young adults in our projects like Food Drives, Towel Drives, etc. Our clubs have several fellowship activities per year that includes family and friends of Rotarians."* He feels the key to continued active membership is to open a line of communication between our club and our members' family.

Phillip Jeffries from Rotary District 7260, writes, *"I firmly believe Rotary does not pay enough attention to the role that family members can play in promoting membership of Rotary. Perhaps the time has come to look at official family membership, an all-inclusive approach to Rotary, and not just a place where Dad or Mom go to serve."*

Time and E-Clubs

It's hard to get younger people involved because everybody is busy. If parents have children to get ready for school, they sometimes fall away from service club meeting attendance. We have a member this year with this problem. In a breakfast club, if both the Rotarian and his partner are working and one of them takes the kids to school, the member may miss the meeting.

In a Rotary International Non-Rotarian Focus Group Comprehensive Report published this year, Rotary stated that most respondents indicated that their time was already stretched beyond acceptable limits and they do not have time to spare.

"Everyone is so time-crunched that we just passed a change in attendance requirements," says Donna McDonald, manager of the Rotary membership development division. *"We're certainly taking people's lifestyles and personal and professional commitments into play."*

E-clubs are one tool to help younger Rotarians with the issue of time. After more than an hour of debate, the 2010 Council on Legislation voted to make e-clubs a permanent part of Rotary International. *"This will allow Rotarians with physical disabilities or [scheduling] restraints to meet regularly and conduct service projects through the Internet,"* said RI Director Antonio Hallage as he presented the proposal to the Council.

Some of the pilot e-clubs meet through online forums, while others combine electronic with in-person meetings. These

Rotary e-clubs have regular fellowship through weekly meetings and other postings in the Members Only Fellowship Forums. As in any Rotary club, they discuss club business, present ideas, share interests, and talk about issues that are important to the club and its members. One of the eClub members said *"Being able to make up meetings on the e-club has helped me to keep perfect attendance."* There are now a number of e-clubs around the world. There are e-clubs in 30 countries and geographical areas, and 586 on-going service e-club projects. E-clubs conduct meetings in Chinese, English, Finnish, Greek, Portuguese, and Spanish.

The Rotary e-Club in District 7890 tells us that their purpose is to extend Rotary to business, professional and community leaders around the world who are unable to meet traditional attendance requirements because extensive travel, conflicting occupational demands, physical immobility, or residence beyond reasonable distance from an existing Rotary Club.

Marco Kappenberger says

> *"The e-clubs permit so very many Rotarians to stay in Rotary, and they do attract so many potential Rotarians who would not have been able to join a traditional Club."*

You might wonder how the e-clubs work on fellowship. Here are a few comments from the Rotary Club of Southwest USA.

"Some people wonder how an e-Club has Fellowship. Actually, we do it just like other clubs. We fly or drive to do projects together, we work together in committees on this website, we share with each other in the forums at every meeting, and we party together."

The club members are heavily engaged in their own communities serving on nonprofit boards, working on youth projects, bringing educational opportunities into local schools to name a few. The club logs over 700 hours of community and international service every month.

New Generations Clubs

New Generations Rotary is a theme for new Rotary clubs that break the mold of a typical morning breakfast or noon meeting.

A New Generations club is focused on making Rotary accessible to a younger generation of working professionals for whom it may be more desirable to meet in an alternative format. The focus of a New Generations Rotary Club is to create something different while still providing "Service Above Self".

Katie Ishkin, president and founder of a New Generation Club in Minneapolis said "We need to focus on generating interest in young people for the future success of Rotary." As a change management consultant, she said she understands people's fear of change. But she stressed that her approach doesn't mean altering the core pieces of the organization or losing what Rotarians hold dear. "What does change are what I call surface-level elements," she said. "The pieces that individual clubs have the power to shift and redesign, such as meeting times and locations, program structures, club member involvement, and committee formats."

Some clubs meet in the evening and they may lowers costs by not having meals. Some clubs only meet every other week. Others hold a happy hour/networking events and the others meet for a hands-on volunteering opportunity. Ischkin added that it's important to understand the mindset of the new generation and manage expectations accordingly. Younger people are "always on the go and truly connected," she explained, whether it's through social networking, text messaging, or other means. They face a lot of pressure to be involved in multiple endeavors and to balance work and personal life. As a result, they may be "on call" with their careers, but they are no less dedicated to service."

"When you're trying to recruit younger members or even sponsor and start a New Generations Rotary club, take time with your club and committee to outline what your expectations are and whether they will align with the younger generation you are trying to attract and work with," she said. "Not every Rotary club can quickly shift gears to attract younger members; it takes time and baby steps." But for many clubs, she said, "all it takes is opening up your minds and starting to think differently about the future of your club's membership."

This section will feature a few of the New Generation clubs in North America.

The **North Orange County New Generations Rotary Club** is a group of 20 to 40 year olds in the heart of Orange County near Disneyland. The focus of the New Generations Rotary Club is to create something different while still providing service. They are ardent in their belief that service comes first, and our good will is spread throughout the community, within other communities such as soldiers in Iraq, those less fortunate and by helping in restoration projects.

The La Jolla New Generation Club in San Diego holds a meeting every Wednesday at 5:30 pm with fellowship and food. Club business and fun starts at 6:00 pm and goes until 7:00 pm. Each week they have an informative speaker presenting interesting topics from their community and world. This New Generations Rotary Club is focused on making Rotary accessible to a younger generation for whom it may be more desirable to meet in the early evenings. Currently the average age of our membership is 31. Each week they have an informative speaker presenting interesting topics of our community and world.

The Rotary Club of Diablo View has 26 members, 90 percent which are between the ages of 25 and 40. They recruit new members through social media like Twitter and Facebook. When the club found it difficult recruit young members they decided to establish a club that meets in a local brewery at 5:30 p.m. every Thursday. Their website tells us that they are a "cocktail hour" club and they provide a relaxed and approachable atmosphere where members and guests can have a bit of mingling before and after the official meeting time. They ask members to come about 5 - 10 minutes early for mingling and getting to know some of the members and guests.

Bricktown Rotary Oklahoma City is a club built around young professionals who are committed to their community, to the ideals of Rotary and to one another. They tell us that their members are doers and that they have at least one service project a month to fill a broad range of needs in Oklahoma City and around the world. They say that they are one of the original "happy hour" clubs and Bricktown tells everyone in their website that they broke through the traditional form of a Rotary Club.

The Rotary Club of South Metro Minneapolis Evenings is a new and young Rotary Club, chartered in June 2010, in the Rotary District of 5950. The club is focused on helping young professionals in the Twin Cities not only get involved in the community both on a local and international level, but to network and meet new people! Their website tells that they are a great group of dynamic and energetic individuals who share one goal – to give back!

Some Clubs Seem Unaware of Membership Problems

Some clubs appear to be unaware of a decline in membership. It's as if they have their head in the sand regarding membership recruitment. One club said

> *"We're all right, thank you, we have enough members and we don't need to recruit."*

It is like a frog. If you place the frog in very cold water and he's a bit uncomfortable, he is very active. If you warm up the water, he goes to sleep. If you continue to heat up the water, he dies and he didn't even see it coming! That's what has been happening to some clubs, and that is what may happen to clubs who take no action. Does this represent your club? Have you ever thought about your club being a frog? Maybe a sleeping frog?

While we may not completely understand why it appears that clubs are not gaining younger members, Putnam in *Bowling Alone*, states that there is "not a general decline in civic engagement, but merely a reorientation from the 'old fashioned' to 'contemporary' affiliations, away from Rotary and the League of Women Voters to Greenpeace and the Sierra Club."

Rotary clubs keep talking about going out and recruiting young people into their ranks. We have heard that young people have been raised with a global awareness of everything from political issues to poverty and the environment. We know they have been expected to volunteer by their parents and their schools and service learning has been on their plate since junior high school days.

We Need to Get the Word Out

In Lancaster's 2010 book, *The M-factor*, she tells us that, *"Many clubs do themselves a disservice by failing to let young people know about the great work they do in making the world a better place."* She says that we should make sure that our web sites, print materials, and even those members recruiting emphasize our contributions to society. Lynne states that *"it's not only Ok to brag, it can be hugely rewarding."* Young people are ready to hear Rotary's stories and it can create valuable social capital with prospective Rotarians as well as with the communities in which we do our volunteer work.

A strong way to get the word out about Rotary is with social media.

Many clubs are working hard these days to stay relevant as a civic networking group. That means embracing Internet tools like social media to recruit young people. You might ask why social media matters.

Just take a look at these numbers.

•57% of all adults have a social media profile.

•50% of all social networkers check their sites every day.

•Twitter use is growing at 400% per year.

•Facebook is the #2 destination on the web.

•The Average Facebook user has 120 friends.

•Over 850 million photos are updated to Facebook each month.

These are numbers that you can't ignore in your Rotary club. Rotary International has developed a presence on Facebook, Twitter and LinkedIn, Flickr, and YouTube.

"The key to recruiting young people into Rotary will be getting the word out in a form that will interest them."

In Paul Kiser's blog on July 28, 2010 Paul made a number of interesting comments that clubs certainly should think about. He stresses the fact that for over thirty years club have relied on the club newsletter as the tool of connection and communication. But today, Paul says "a newsletter is only slightly higher on the value scale than junk mail." The problem he states is that few people have time to spend 15 minutes reading it and much of the information is not of interest to the reader. Enter Facebook and Twitter. Paul tells us that most of the clubs that he has been involved in regarding incorporating Facebook or Twitter into club communications have included this statement, "But most of our club members don't use Facebook."

"If there is a defining remark about the state of a club's recruitment situation, that is it".

Kiser states that "over 500 million people use Facebook and Rotary clubs don't think it is relevant because their current members don't use it. If your membership is not using the most current methods of communication, that should tell you why people in the real world see Rotary and your club as out-of-date and out of touch." The club Kiser strongly stresses "that doesn't have an active website and Facebook Fan Page within 12 months will most likely be the club that is consistently struggling to maintain membership. It's that simple."

Paul Harris began Rotary to make connections with other people. Paul Harris would have loved Social Media.

Since the younger people tell us that they do not read print media, we will need to use these newer forms of social technology to reach them. Most of us know online social networking is a big deal, but don't know what to do about it. A few of us use Facebook in our personal lives but aren't quite sure how it fits with Rotary.

If we do not understand social media and you have kids, just go down the hall and watch them for a while. If you don't have kids of your own, spend some time with a friend's kids. Watch them playing, communicating, and learning. Notice how much of their lives are being spent on line. Just visit an Apple store to watch the little ones play with technology. According to Clara Shih in her book, *The Facebook Era*,

"Thanks to their viral nature, we have reached the tipping point in the mass adoption of online social networks, and they will only continue growing in prominence and pervasiveness."

It would be hard to find anyone in high school or college without a Facebook page. According to Facebook, although it maintains an 85 percent or greater penetration among four-year U.S. universities, more than half of its users are out of college, and those 35 and older represent the fastest-growing demographic. Winogread in his book *Millennial Makeover*, tells us that *"younger voters are twice as likely as others to use the net, rather than the newspapers, to get information about political campaigns."*

The most recent US Presidential election demonstrated that the use of social networking sites, such as MySpace, Facebook, and You Tube as a political recruiting tool. We can learn a great deal from Barack Obama's 2008 presidential campaign, which used Facebook, MySpace and other social networking sites to rally millions of supporters and helped raise nearly $1 billion in grassroots campaign contributions.

According to the Pew Research Center, 10 percent of Americans used Facebook or another social networking site to get information about the presidential election. This includes one-third of Americans under the age of thirty.

"If the Xers and Millennials are the connected generation, then Rotary needs to become the connected club."

Rotary has joined the connected era with its social networking sites. The Rotary website says it best when it states, *"Rotarians help provide service through fellowship, and social networking is one of the many ways Rotarians are connecting online."*

According to the Cone Study, the bottom line is that the best way for organizations to reach young people with cause-related messages is to redefine the marketing experience. This

Cone study found that when a cause message is linked to a brand in an authentic and relevant way, it can gain the attention and respect of young people today. Furthermore, a shared passion for a cause can foster a strong personal relationship between a brand and its target consumer. Younger adults are ready to reward or punish an organization depending on its commitment to social and/or environmental causes. Cause marketing should be considered as a loyalty strategy for engaging them.

The result of this study appears to suggest that young members will foster a strong relationship with Rotary only if they feel strongly about the service projects that the club is undertaking.

In fact, according to the study if they do not agree with the cause, they will likely fail to support the club based on their personal feelings. That makes it critical that we find those causes that today's young adults in fact are willing to support.

Recruiting Young People and Change

RI President Bill Boyd said it so correctly when he said "If we don't get enough young people in Rotary, then Rotary will die." A very strong statement, but a true one indeed. If our membership base is 89% members over the age of 40 and many of the older members are going to pass away in the next decade, where does that leave us?

> *"It is very interesting that when Paul Harris started Rotary in 1905, the original four members were in their late thirties and early forties."*

Rotary is now putting an increased emphasis in the RI Membership Development Division to better target younger professionals ages, 30-45 years of age. The reasons why Rotary is attempting to focus on bringing younger members includes the following from a Rotarian Focus Group in Los Angeles in June, 2008:

- They bring the energy/strength of youth.

- They bring a new vision to the club.

- They help to introduce newer technology to the club.

- Their impact increases the number and frequency of club social activities.

- They bring great ideas for club program speakers and expand the club's contacts and network.

- They can bring the club closer to the community because they have more current contacts within the community.

- They can be a source of greater ethnic diversity.

- They provide for the "perpetuity of the club."

Why Don't Young People Join Rotary?

There are many reasons given for why younger people don't join Rotary.

"But the most critical reason that younger people don't join is that they don't know anything about Rotary."

I know that when I aged out as the President of the Yorba Linda Jaycees, which occurred at about 30 years old, I really did not know about Rotary. I knew that there was a Rotary club in town but it seemed that this was for those older and much more successful men in town. The truth is that I did not ask and probably much more importantly, no one asked me to come visit a Rotary club. It took me years to discover the value of a Rotary membership.

Why is it that the majority of Rotary members do not actively recruit new members? Well, these members attend the weekly Rotary meeting, listen to the Membership Minute, and go back to work after the meeting. But, when they talk to a fellow professional, it never occurs to them to talk about Rotary. They might even talk about a Rotary project, but they fail to suggest that their friend join Rotary.

We all have to **focus** on membership in order to be stronger recruiters. What does focus mean? I means thinking about membership recruiting. I think of Stephen Covey's classic text, *7 Habits of Highly Effective People* where he discusses the three steps of seeing, doing, and getting. This is so clear to me. You first must learn to see a prospective member. Then you must do the Rotary ask of inviting them to be your guest at a Rotary meeting. And lastly, you must get that prospect into the Rotary club.

"Recruiting new members of any age is easy, but only if we focus on recruiting".

The key to recruiting anyone is figuring out why someone is interested in joining. There are a number of reasons that members join Rotary. The top six would include networking, social, learning, recognition, fun, and service.

Networking is the same as building fellowship and that is a strong reason that people join Rotary. The chamber has as its major purpose to increase business and increase business contacts. The truth is that you only increase business contacts by increasing fellowship. Many members feel that Rotary is not a networking club. They think of networking clubs like BNI or LeTip. True, networking is not our prime purpose but it is a major help for many of your members. It works so well because of the Four Way Test. In other words, we trust each other and have no fear of recommending a member to anyone.

Social as a reason for joining Rotary means that your club works hard on fellowship activities. Many people join when they are new to a community and it is a key way to meet fellow professionals in the community. You will find that you tend to develop and grow strong relationships with fellow Rotarians and their families.

Learning is critical to our younger members as they join to develop their resumes and develop meaningful learning relationships. The weekly program is a wonderful source of knowledge to be gained from the programs given by outstanding speakers. This is why it is so important to generate an outstanding roster of speakers for your club. Members check out the weekly newsletter to decide if they will be inviting guests for the program.

Recognition is critical to every professional business person. Many industries do not do a strong job of rewarding their employees. It is simply a matter of saying thank you and patting your members on their backs. Rotary is very strong about giving recognition for work well done.

Fun is probably the strongest need for every member. If the club meeting and the service projects are not fun then members will lose interest. Social activities that involve the whole family need to have fun as a prime attribute of the event. We all work hard at arranging fundraising and service activities therefore you need to insure that they are fun as well.

Service goes without much explanation as this is the number one venture of any Rotary club. We arrange both community and international service activities. It is through the pictures following a service activity that we get that good feeling about all that hard work we gave. It is always fun to see pictures of our club service in the local newspaper or on television. True "Service Above Self" projects are the key to Rotary recruitment and retention.

Many members attend membership seminars to try and find the secrets to membership recruiting. There truly are no secrets to recruiting but there is the opportunity to apply a few very simple techniques. Whenever you attend any community function, you have an opportunity to market your Rotary passion. You need to learn about your prospects experiences, personality, and priorities so that you don't waste each other's time talking about something that doesn't appeal to them. Your words will not convince people to join Rotary. The more time you spend talking, the less time they will spend listening. The faster you talk, the more desperate you will sound. Give just enough information about Rotary to help excite the prospect in attending lunch or breakfast with you.

You need to approach every ask from your prospect's perspective. This first meeting is the time to connect with your prospect and for them to connect with you. The fastest way to connect is to show a genuine interest in your prospect's life.

Ask about their family and friends. Find the prospect's passion and interests. Ask about their career and educational background.

When you show that you are interested in them, they will begin to show an interest in you.

Many people are afraid that they do not have all the answers about Rotary or that the prospect will ask a question they cannot answer. It is always a good to say simply, that you don't know the answer but that you will find out and get back to them. A simple call to your club president or assistant governor will find the answer. Then you can call your prospect with the answer. It will impress them that you cared enough to spend the time to find the best answer to their question.

Recruiting Requires Focus

Most of us want to recruit new members, but we simply either don't know how or we just fail to think about it at the right time. I like to think that we fail to "focus" on recruiting.

I say that because each of us meet about a dozen potential members every day. You go into the super market, the bank, the shoe repair shop and your dentist. We do all these tasks or maybe they are on our "honey-do " lists. We are simply getting the job done and probably we are warm and friendly to the people we meet. But we fail to see them all as potential members.

When is the last time you thought about asking your banker or super market manager to consider joining your club?

You see them regularly but when we discuss recruiting, they don't seem to pop into your mind. That is because when you go into these businesses, you are not thinking membership. You also don't have a club brochure in your pocket or purse. You don't have that little card inviting the person to be your guest for lunch or breakfast. Remember when your club had those printed and gave you a stack of them? It would be a good exercise during a meeting to have each member think of three people that they might give those cards to and ask to be their guest at a meeting.

It is important to think of inviting someone to be your guest for a meal at your club. It is much better to invite them to share a meal than to invite them to a meeting. Most of us have way too many meetings to attend. But to share a meal with a friend, even a brand new one, is more interesting.

It puts no pressure on the person. In fact, give them very little information about your club, except to say we do service to help our community. I find that if I over push the club message at that first meeting, it's not as effective as going light with the sales pitch. They are usually impressed with all that the club represents after they meet my fellow club members. I do mention a project that we are doing to help our local community. I might focus on helping kids if the person is younger or I might talk about our senior care projects if they are older.

In other words I am going to focus on what I think their personal "hot button" might be.

Usually, you gather this information after a short conversation with them as you listen to talk about what their interests are. We might take a good look at our club first. You are asking potential new members to join, so what would be the attraction for them? Do you have strong fellowship, an outstanding venue, a program of interesting speakers, meaningful hands-on projects? Do you meet at a convenient time? These are important questions to consider.

Recruiting is such a simple process, but so complex for some members to understand. It is simply a matter of asking another person to join. But that requires you to think about it. It appears that many members simply do not focus on recruiting during their visits with friends and business contacts. It is a problem to find prospective members for some, and for others, it is being able to ask.

One of our members says that he will be forever grateful to the lady who introduced him to Rotary. He says, *"her enthusiasm and love of Rotary is something I carry with me at all times."* Our member's goal is to emulate her... to 'share the gift of Rotary' with all the people he knows.

He says,

"It never hurts to invite someone to lunch when you offer more than just a meal! You offer the opportunity to make a difference in our world!"

Bill Pollard, PDG of District 7600 was very clear in this statement, *"To me it is pretty simple. Someone thought enough of you to invite you to a Rotary meeting. If being a Rotarian has had a positive impact on your professional and personal career, then the best thing you can do for Rotary is to help grow our family."*

For example, when you attend a chamber of commerce mixer you have an opportunity to meet and greet other local professionals from your community. I know you go to the mixer and shake hands with a variety of professionals each month. You even share business cards with these professionals, but many of us forget to mention Rotary? I am as guilty as the rest of you. See, I fail to focus on Rotary myself at times.

"You need to walk into the event with the goal of finding one new professional and inviting them to your Rotary club."

When you locate a fellow professional, introduce yourself and after a few minutes, ask them "why aren't you a member of Rotary?" This is a very simple question and after thinking about it you will get one of two responses, first, they might say that they have heard about Rotary, but they have no idea what they are. Or very likely, they will say that they have never been asked to join. Either way, they are ready for a short Rotary talk from you. You might consider this Rotary talk as your elevator speech. An elevator speech is usually a short (45 minute – two minute) presentation where you explain the good work that Rotary performs.

The key to getting them to consider joining Rotary is to have them attend a club meeting as your guest. It is best if you don't just invite them to a meeting. Nobody today wants to attend one more meeting. Most of us consider meetings to be boring. Invite them to breakfast or lunch or dinner, depending on your club meeting times. Offer to pay for their meal. Have them give you their e-mail address. Send them a reminder of the invitation that same day. Tell them about the program that you are inviting them to as your guest. Have your club add them to your club mailing list.

Do not be hurt if your invitation goes without a solid positive response. Many people will be too busy right now to attend, but will consider at a later date, if you keep them on the newsletter list.

Use an e-mailing program like Constant Contact for your e-newsletter mailing company. Constant Contact will let you check to see if the prospect has opened the newsletter, I am happily surprised to see that they do open it each week. Then send a friendly reminder to them with another warm introduction and invitation for them to be your guest at Rotary.

Another location to search for new members is your local businesses. Every one of us goes into a number of businesses each day and on weekends. These businesses are each a location with many professionals who might be interested in Rotary. You walk into your bank branch. Do you know the manager? Have you asked the manager to be your guest at Rotary? One of the managers that I asked took me over 2 years to sign up as a new member. Just because someone says no at first does not mean no for life. Sometimes people need the right time and situation to say yes.

According to Rotary International, most Rotarians (82% based on latest RI survey) never propose a new member.

It is important for you to carry a membership application in your coat or purse at all times. A business card with a personal invitation on the back of it would be helpful too. You might put a label on the back of your professional business card. The label will invite them to whatever meal your club holds as its meeting. Always know who the speaker is for your next Rotary meeting. It makes sense to invite your guest to gain knowledge or fun with you at the next meeting.

Why Is It So Difficult To Bring Younger People Into Rotary?

Younger people might prefer a more comfortable and relaxed environment where they can still have fun and get things done. They do not like meetings, at work or in social settings. They prefer events that get to the point and accomplish something fast. They consider meetings a waste of time unless they are fun and well organized.

Many younger professionals may be intimidated or turned-off by the formality and ritual associated with many Rotary clubs.

The first thing many of these young professionals ask me during my membership visit is "How much does Rotary cost?" They will sometimes say that they think that Rotary is a "Rich man's group." The cost of Rotary scares many young professionals. You might tell them the cost of Rotary club and district dues. But that is usually not the largest cost of Rotary membership. It is the meal cost and fines and foundation fundraising. Many clubs are considering offering a reduced dues structure for younger professionals. They even allow those members to purchase off the menu to avoid high costs.

Many times our younger member's tell their friends that they have joined Rotary, and their friends say "But you are too young for Rotary."

There is an assumption that Rotarians are older. This maybe an unfair view that Rotarians are all older, but it is a reaction that many young people may feel. We should view bringing younger people into Rotary the same way professional sports teams view the minor leagues. We need "bench strength" built into our clubs. You go to a professional baseball game and you see all those young players sitting on the bench waiting for their turn to come onto the playing field. These young plays in their clean uniforms are the future of the team. We need new players on our Rotary team to help us move into our second hundred years of Rotary.

Michael McQueen, a speaker on Generation Y at the recent International Convention in New Orleans points out two questions that young people have about Rotary. First is the question, why do we do it that way? They might ask why we start the meeting by ringing a bell, why we say grace, why is it called 'fellowship' and according to McQueen, the list goes on.

McQueen suggests that we should not perceive this questioning as a threat or challenge to the status quo. Maybe we do not always know why we do certain things in Rotary. Maybe its just always been done that way. But these younger members are curious. Give them the best answers you can.

The second question that McQueen suggests that young members will ask is why we do it at all. Why do we sing a song that is so old that they never heard it before? Why a bell? Why do we fine each other? These are all traditions in your club and maybe you need to find the reason that we do these things.

Why do the young members join? They are attracted to clubs because of the benefits and outcomes that membership will lead to. They are simply asking why we exist as a Rotary club, what are we achieving, who are we helping.

They are not joining Rotary simply to become a club member.

Remember that young members are looking to do something in Rotary. It's why they join. They do not want to just attend meetings once a week. They are action-oriented and they want to make a difference in their community and across the world.

What Changes Might a Club Consider To Make Rotary More Inviting To Young People?

When asked what our clubs may change to make Rotary more inviting, here are a few suggestions from a wide variety of clubs.

- Switch to an evening format with only optional beverages and hors d'oeuvres.

- Make sure the meetings are interesting and to-the-point.

- Ease up on some of the rules and expectations for attendance.

- Reduce some of the formality in meetings.

- Invite Rotary alumni to attend your club.

- Start new clubs with either all younger members or a more even age balance.

- Work with the media to change the image of Rotary from being an "old person's club."

Many of the younger professional stated that they do not want any membership rules or expectations changed for them. They want to be full Rotarians but that they hope that the clubs will consider making it easier for all Rotarians to meet attendance and monetary requirements in this difficult economy.

How Easy Is It To Find Information About Your Club?

You won't attract members if information about your club is not easily accessible.

In today's world most people will go online to find something they are interested in. It's important then that your club has a clear and up to date website for them to view. This website should contain the answers to the questions they are most likely to ask.

At a minimum it should provide information on:

What your club is about - What is your mission statement? What future goals are you aiming for? What past achievements are you proud of? How old is the club? How many members does the club have? What is the average age of your members? How many women are club members?

Your club's membership requirements - Are there any restrictions on who can join? What is expected of a member?

Are there attendance requirements? What does it cost to be a member?

What service projects do the club focus on? When are they coming up on your club's calendar? What is involved in these projects? Can family and friends help on projects?

When and where does your club meet? How long does a club meeting last? What can a visitor expect at a club meeting? What time do your start? What day is the meeting on?

Who should a potential member contact if they wish to attend a meeting or get involved in a project? Who is the membership contact? Who is the club president?

Once you've managed to entice a potential member to attend a club meeting or event, it's very important to make them feel welcome.

Acknowledge their presence, extend a friendly welcome to them and make them feel a part of what's going on. It can be very helpful to assign a "buddy" who can answer any questions or explain things as they come up.

As for the meeting itself, it's important to keep the meeting vibrant and flowing. This is just as important for the retention of existing members as for the attraction of new ones. All business meetings can get quite boring and may put visitors off. Try to keep the business brief and always have a guest speaker to cover an interesting topic. Be sure to include time for fellowship, before, after and during breaks in the meeting.

It's shocking how many clubs are holding back their potential members by excluding whole groups of people. The most obvious form of exclusion is that based on age or gender. Potential prospects could be being excluded because of pre-conceived ideas or stereotyping. For example, you may be excluding university students because they are too transient. Another common one is not asking older, experienced and retired professional people. Clubs may have a bias against younger members that shows up by not allowing them to join into a conversation. Or you might restrict them from sitting at a certain table which by tradition has belonged to a certain group of old timers.

The Starbucks Approach to Finding Young Prospects

I am known around my district as the Starbucks Guy since I spend so much time at Starbucks recruiting Rotarians. Why Starbucks? Well think about the concept and brand of

Starbucks. Starbucks has over the years created its own culture of the new age for twenty and thirty something year olds. Who ever thought one could combine computers, the Internet and that strong, cup of coffee. Starbucks has so cleverly and craftily managed to do this.

Starbucks has become 'the new culture' in coffee drinking. The market aims at busy, young professionals. The vibrant atmosphere of the Starbucks coffee shops makes it quite popular for young, single people. Busy working class people also like to sometimes stop by just to surf the Internet on their laptops, and also have some coffee. Robert Woolf, A 29-year-old ad writer in Parsippany, N.J., spends $40 a week on Starbucks lattes. Gas prices are climbing, though, and his salary isn't, still, Woolf won't be turning to Maxwell House or Folgers for his fix.

"I don't know anyone outside my Dad's Lions Club who drinks that stuff."

This target market is mostly comprised of young professionals, who typically have higher incomes, and stressful jobs. Most live in suburban areas, but commute to urban areas daily. Starbucks core customers stop in before or after work for a pick-me- up. Does this target market sound like prospective Rotarians? They are young up and coming professional business people ripe for an opportunity to think Rotary.

I always stop by Starbucks near where my Rotary club meets for breakfast. So following our meeting, my wife and I, and three other Rotarians arrive for a mocha. As I sat down with my drink and friends, I notice a young woman walk in the door. I tap my wife on the shoulder and ask her if that is one. By one, I mean, is that a prospect that we should approach about Rotary? She said yes and I asked her if this prospect is mine, or hers. She laughs and says that she got the last one so I should ask this person about Rotary. First of all, I do not approach people who appear to be in a rush to get to work, and I have not yet figured how to work the drive-though line. I get up and carefully approach this young professional by asking her a simple, but effective question.

"Why aren't you a Rotarian?"

I talk about the service that my Rotary club performs in our local community. I do not stress the international service because most people are excited about service where we live. After I get these people into Rotary, I will work them into international service. Most people are excited when they hear that Rotary supports children, teens, seniors and a variety of local charities.

Just how good am I at recruiting these young professionals? Well I invite about ten people to get one to join. Is that good or bad? I think it is wonderful because in all sales it takes a number of no's to get a good solid yes. Think about it this way, it takes a number of asks to get a sale. This Starbucks Approach has helped our club to grow from seven to fifty-three in just over two years. Starbucks is but one example, but the key to my message is that you need to find people where they are. Where are young professionals to be found? Where do they hang out? Figure that out and go there to give your Rotary talk.

Why Did You Join Rotary?

It is critical for each of us to consider the reason that we first joined a service club. I am sure if you have eighteen members in your club, you will have at least eighteen different reasons why your members joined.

My reason was fairly typical. My wife and I moved to Elk Grove from Southern California because our daughter and her husband settled there. We had lived in Southern California for many years, and we wanted to be near that upcoming grand-child. Upon arriving in Elk Grove we soon realized that every friend we had in the world, except for the daughter, was now 500 miles south of us. So during the first week in town, I read in the Elk Grove Citizen that a group called Rotary was having a Wine Tasting/Garage Sale on Saturday. So, on Saturday, we went to that Wine Tasting/Garage Sale event. It sounded interesting since I like wine and my wife is a garage sale addict.

When we arrived to taste and buy, we met a number of those so-called "Rotarians." They were warm and friendly and they talked to me about this "Rotary" organization. I had heard about Rotary, and it seemed like one of those elite organizations full of important people. Maybe just what I needed to become involved in this new town I moved into. I thought this an opportunity to meet those movers and shakers and at the same time do the service that they talked about.

As I think back to that day, actually no one asked me to join. Oh well. But now I was the new kid and since I didn't know anyone in town it might be time to check out this club. These Rotary guys seemed friendly enough and they had invited me to a meeting for lunch on Wednesday. But Wednesday came and went and I did not go to the meeting. On the following week, I got a phone call from one of those Rotarians re-inviting me to sample their meeting. I did attend and within a few weeks, I was asked to join the club. I sort of expected a "secret handshake" or something, but it was just a group of local men and women business professionals who were doing a number of meaningful community service projects.

I joined for my reason, to meet new people. In Rotary talk, I joined for fellowship. As I explored Rotary, I found that a founding principle of Rotary was to meet periodically to enjoy camaraderie and enlarge one's circle of business and professional acquaintances.

The Rotary booklet said that,

"As the oldest service club in the world, Rotary club members represent a cross-section of the community's owners, executives, managers, political leaders, and professionals – people who make decisions and influence policy."

That was exactly what I was looking for. I think I might have joined any service club that offered me their hand, but Rotary asked first.

Why Do Other People Join Rotary?

It is important to realize that people join a service club for many different reasons. It is a good exercise at a club meeting to ask each member, why they joined. They might not even remember why they joined, but as you go around the room, they will sense the reason they said Yes, I will join this club.

What happens at the meeting and how they are treated has so much to do with whether they just enjoyed a single meal and moved on or whether they came back for a second visit.

Very little depends on where you meet, be it a Denny's Restaurant or the country club. But, your club does need a plan to get prospects involved right from the start. I find it helps to invite the prospect to a social event with families, or to a hands-on work project. A recent study revealed that the more involved members are in club activities, the happier and more fulfilled they are with the club experience.

I am thinking about a brand new member that my wife invited to our club. He was a fellow church member and in fact, he and his wife were in our church Diner's Club. They were very warm people and I think his wife was more out-going than he, but he liked wine and maybe that was my connection. He had recently retired as a contractor because of knee problems, and was spending much of his day at home watching that bright tube called television. He loved ball games and there he sat most days. His wife said he should join something, but he was not interested in the least. They knew that my wife and I were both involved in Rotary and in fact I was the incoming president and she, the club secretary. We invited him to be our guest for breakfast and I could tell that was not the best offer he had had that week. But we kept suggesting he attend, and sure enough, maybe out of a desire to have us stop asking, he did show up.

It was a nice surprise when he showed up for a club meeting, and he came a few more times and picked up an application. After three breakfasts, he joined and has not missed a meeting since, and he is working on a number of service projects. I hope my point is clear, first, all we did is to offer him an opportunity to be our guest for breakfast. No requirement to do anything except show up and enjoy breakfast. Our members all introduced themselves to him and were interested to learn that he was a contractor. That gave everyone an opportunity to have a conversation with him.

I think he felt important as people were asking him questions about his career. He was not introduced as a prospective member, just as a guest. That took any pressure off. He was told that he could attend and have a free breakfast for as long as he wished. Our club gives that offer to all prospects, but very few people stay for more than 2-3 weeks before joining. He decided to join after being invited to work on a hands-on project. I think he joined for two reasons, first it gave him something meaningful to do with his time, and secondly, he found a whole new group of interesting friends.

What Words Describe Rotarians?

It is interesting to see in the recent Rotary International Non-Rotarian Focus Group Report, most people are unaware of what Rotary gets involved with, or what Rotary stands for. In general, there was a significant lack of awareness as to what Rotary International or local Rotary clubs accomplish. Some indicated, "they have that wheel." When asked about their perception of Rotary, the following words were used to characterize Rotary and Rotarians:

Business men
Elite
Secretive

Older Wealthy
Not 'sexy'
Not 'trendy'
Inflexible
Not sure that women are allowed into local clubs

It appears from this survey that many people have a significant lack of knowledge of what Rotary actually does, what Rotary accomplishes within the local community or internationally, or how one would get involved in or engaged with Rotary's efforts.

It is apparent that many people had no image of Rotary at all.

It seems that many prospects are unable to gather information about Rotary. The Rotary Focus Group also said that *"individuals mentioned that they were interested in the organization and had attempted to contact a club but there was no follow-up on the club's behalf, or the club informed them that their classification was filled."* They also said that they had attempted to locate a website for the club but could not find one.

What Is The Number One Reason That People Join Rotary?

They became Rotarians because someone asked them.

The overwhelming majority of people never considered Rotary before they were approached. That is not surprising. Rotary operates by invitation. We don't run media campaigns trumpeting our opportunity and we don't advertise in the newspaper. Unless and until you connect with your prospects, how will they know how incredible the opportunity is?

These prospects are not going to come knocking on your door. You have to reach out to them--preferably before someone from another service club does.

 Approach people and talk about Rotary at every opportunity you get. If the opportunity doesn't present itself, create one. The more people you talk to, the more successful you will be.

What is the Percentage of Women in your Club?

A major concern in is that many clubs have an extremely small number of women or even no women members. Rotary was without female members until 1989. That is when the Rotary Council on Legislation voted to change the Constitution and By-laws to permit the admission of women into Rotary. Now Rotary has a number of women as members and many of those are from the mature generation.

In the United States the average number of women Rotarians equals about 28 percent of club membership

This is not very high when you consider the number of women managers and corporate CEOs. There are an estimated 10.1 million majority-owned, privately-held, women-owned firms in the U.S.. Women-owned businesses account for 28 percent of all businesses in the United States and account for 55 percent of new startups. Women-owned firms grew by 19.8 percent while all U.S. firms grew by seven percent. Rotary has nearly 200,000 female Rotarians and women have served in leadership positions as high as the RI Board of Directors and The Rotary Foundation Board of Trustees. There are currently sixty-three serving as district governors.

Penny Shurtleff, Rotary Club of La Jolla gives us insight into the feelings of a Rotarian woman member. *"I was one of the first women in my club in Santa Rosa, CA. The male Rotarians were very accepting of me. Although they tested me by giving me every job there was to do to prove myself, I met the challenge and earned their respect"*

According to Past District Governor Talee Crowe of District 5450,

"The addition of women in Rotary represents the single greatest force in the growth of Rotary International."

Most Rotarians and Rotary Clubs know first-hand the powerful impact that bringing women into their membership has made on the work of our organization. The participation of women in Rotary International has resulted in clubs across the world giving more attention to and raising more funds for women's issues, especially domestic violence, education for young girls and women in developing countries, and the need for basic health care for poor women and children around the globe.

If you consider the tremendous growth of women into the work world then the slow growth of women into some Rotary clubs needs to be evaluated.

Just 20 years ago, the Rotary Club was a bastion of "men only" exclusion. Women, banned from membership, were relegated to secondary citizenship as "Rotary Ann" associates. Now, less than a generation later, Rotary roles are reversing where women often run the show. Out of 33,790 Rotary clubs worldwide, 26,853 has at least one woman as a member for a total of 80% of all Rotary clubs having women members.

"As the women came in, they brought in women," said Joan Gagnon, president of the Foxborough Rotary Club. "The dynamics in America have changed," said Suzanne Kavanagh , president of the Scituate Rotary Club, which has the highest concentration of women in the area. *"My father would tell me stories about how, in the 1930s and 1940s, while the wife was at home, the man would belong to five clubs -- the Elks Club, the Moose Club, the Lions Club, VFW -- and would be out of the house five nights a week. Now, with the wife at work and with kids at soccer practice, it's not possible."*

When Teri Fitch of Newport, R.I., took the podium as district governor in 2007, she gave a few fun thoughts, *"there are no women, and no men, only Rotarians"*

A Few Closing Thoughts

Rotary is a great organization and one that all of its members are proud to be a part of. But unless we continue to grow its membership base it may not be here in the next generation.

"We will become a stagnant organization unless we are willing to get out and find new members for Rotary."

We are doing well at building bridges across the world with our service above self. We need to start building bridges across generations as well. We need to bring a strong sense of diversity into Rotary. This diversity means more gender and age diversity. We are doing well in attracting women into our clubs, but we can certainly do better. We certainly know we must bring younger people into Rotary even if that means some changes need to occur in Rotary.

Membership is every members job. Only a few club members ever ask anyone to join their club. I believe that most Rotarians plan to ask a friend to join Rotary. But they do not ask for any of a number of reasons. Maybe they are afraid the person will say no and they will feel rejection. Maybe they are afraid that the person will ask a question that they do not know the answer to. Maybe they just never find the 'best' time to ask.

The past Rotary theme of "Membership is Everyone's Job" certainly hit the nail on the head. If we are going to grow our club then we need to help every member to ask someone to consider Rotary. We can start this membership process by asking ourselves why we joined Rotary and if we are still enjoying Rotary. I think a lot of our early thoughts about Rotary had a lot to do with the fact that someone thought enough of us to invite us to Rotary.

It was a special moment when a friend invited us to their Rotary club.

It's our opportunity to make this special feeling for someone that we invite into Rotary.

If you would like to have Dr. Bill Wittich speak at one of your events, please contact him at :

Dr. Bill Wittich

8650 Heritage Hill Drive

Elk Grove, California 95624

916.601.2485 cell

billwittich@comcast.net e-mail

www.billwittich.com   website

His print publications are available at

www. Amazon.com

This book is available in e-book formats at www. energizeinc.com and from the Apple ibook store.